AUTUMN IN HER VEINS

TANNU SHREE

ISBN 979-888569312-7

Contents

Contents

Contents

Contents

Acknowledgements

I gave almost 8 months to this book and finally it's here. First of all, I would like to express my gratitude and thank everyone who helped me to complete this book.

I would like to thank my parents for standing through every rain and shin, they always encouraged me to write even when I was on the urge of giving up and they are the ones who has always been a constant support in all shades of my life, my siblings and my friends and each and every one who has never let the fire die inside me and made me believe in myself.

I would also want to thank my teacher Ms. Ayushi Zina Ma'am for reviewing my book, thank you for the guidance, under you we're being able to come out with the best versions of ourselves especially as writers.

I would like to thank each other for not assassinating my dreams and for not giving up on this book.

And lastly, I would like to thank all my lovely readers for whom I have penned all the words.

1. BITE ON MY SKIN

"Now when I try to recall those old days I get goosebumps because it feels like you injected poison each time you bite my skin..."

2. NOW I KNOW

We ran away from our mistakes.
now i realize why you were running away from me.

3. LONGING

I long for a love.
a love in which we can dance
to the rhythm of serenity.

4. NOT ABOUT TIME

They say, that time heals.
but it's been a long long time since i got my heart broken
and my wounds you know?
they still bleed.

5. NO

Would you like to have your true love's kiss for one last time?

no

why?

would you give a thirsty traveler just a drop of water and then walk

away?

6. CHEST ON GRENADE

I carry a chest that feels so heavy.
and a mind with thoughts that are messy.
I don't remember when i last felt light
when it last felt right
when you last held me tight
told me it's going to be alright
when you last were polite
when i last didn't cry myself to sleep at night.
I carry a chest that feels so heavy.
and a mind with thoughts that are messy.

7. NEED WARMTH NOT BRUISES

Someone said that "I love you" is a feeling that always stays,
But it's better to put an end to those feelings when instead of warmth it
gives you bruises...
So, it's okay to weep for few nights rather than spending your entire life
carrying those burden.

8. DIFFERENCES...

"Let's have some shots of love, light some cigar and just blow our differences..."

9. TALE

"You know what's worst when the favourite tale of your life go round in circles and turns out to be the worst of all...."

10. IRONY

What's the worst but yet the most aesthetic way to describe a love story?
compare it to the autumn.
people find it beautiful, even when everything's dying.

11. CONTAMINATED LOVE

Ah! today I found a letter which says:
"You mean the whole world to me and I'll always be your side no matter
what the situation is..." this reminds me how beautifully you
contaminated this pure feeling called love with your lies...

12. BLESSING OR CURSE?

All I ever wanted to experience from love was the blessing of heaven but falling for you came to me as a curse of hell...

13. BITTERNESS FOR BETTERMENT

"Tough times are like bitter gourd first it spoils your taste buds by it's bitterness, but in order to make things work for your betterment ..."

14. WHEN THE WORLD FALL APART

"The worst thing that can happen in one's life is when they are watching their whole world fall apart, and all they can do is to stare blankly."

15. BROKEN? FIX IT.

Even if I fall and break into pieces,
Choose to gather all my courage and
fix myself...

16. MAN OF HIS OWN WORDS

"It's better to be alone and live a peaceful life rather than being stuck with a spineless person who can't even be a man of his own words..."

17. COSMIC LOVERS

A cosmic bouquet from me to you,
Maybe you didn't expect it to happen where I jumped in your balcony
holding flowers in my hands with a smile on my face and it turning out
to be something that came out of blue.
You got my heart go wild that made me love your every move,
With some dim lights and soft tunes that's driving both of us away from
this chaotic buss and we as lovers creating our cosmic love....

18. YOU ARE ENOUGH

"You are enough,
Even if you are broken and can't find some of your pieces.
You are enough... "

19. AUTUMN IN HER VEINS

There's autumn in her veins,
Like deciduous tree shedding its leaves of happiness and still feels no pain.
As those beautiful leaves changing from green to red, orange, yellow or
brown before falling and dying on the ground,
Though she feels like someone has rubbed salt in her wound, she still has
the courage to gather all her strength and come back to the battleground.
As the daylight starts growing shorter, the temperature grows colder,
But there's one thing for sure that its beauty can be seen only in the eyes of
the beholder...

20. I'M SORRY WINTER

Sorry winter that i blamed you for cold
because i never knew that there are people around us
that can make us feel dead from inside,
sorry those dead leaves on the streets for calling you lifeless
without knowing your struggle and efforts in making the world
look green as i failed to understand that
there are people who can swallow your happiness
in order to satisfy their pride.

21. GO

go make magic in people's lives
because someone made magic in yours.
go love someone a sweet as you can
because someone loved you before.
go lend a generous hand
because someone gave you a little more.
go be kind to a downtrodden soul

22. THINK, THOUGHT, THROUGH

"Did you think this through?" she said.
"No. i only thought of you." he said.

23. I BEGGED

I begged you to stay.
But you ignored all my pleads.
You blamed me for not understanding you.
Still I never questioned you ever for all your deeds.
But that day when I ran after you on the road just to have a conversation
for five minutes and you denied for that.
That has left an imprint on my heart and mind.
That day I felt as if my heart was crushed and thrown away.
You promised me that you'll hold my hands no matter what but when it
was time to actually prove you left me when I needed you the most and
now I'm left drained and cold...

24. I SIT, I STAND, I MOVE, READY

I sit serene

I sit quiet

I sit knowing there is more

I sit waiting, ready to want more

I stand tall

I stand still

I stand knowing no direction

I stand turning, ready to move on

I move forward

I move away

I move taking on a path

I move hoping, ready to seek forth.

25. LIES

"Stop swallowing any more of his lies..."

26. CRY

I wanna cry.

Cry out loud because I know that I'm holding a storm inside and that's
making me cold with each day passing by.

I wanna set myself free,

Free from all chains of pains because I know how tough it is to rise ever
morning even when my body aches.

It's been a long time since I have genuinely smiled because I'm still trying
to fix myself since you have broken me into pieces.

27. LOVE FLIES

When I hesitated on the first to believe in a beautiful thing called 'love',
You clutched my hands tightly and made me feel those love flies inside my
tummy.
And when it seemed to me as my home,
You abandoned me without any reason.

28. YOU CALL IT WHAT YOU WANT

When she mention it for the first time, You say she's complaining.
When she brings it up twice,
You say she's nagging and continuously poking you.
When she weeps and cry her heart out,
You label her as being too sensitive and over dramatic.
Hello my good friend, let me ask you this, when she leaves... What will
you call her then?

29. LIFE LESS THAN DEATH

She is not sad.
but exactly she's not happy either.
She can fake smile whole day
and pretend like she's the happiest person alive.
But when she's alone
at night she forgets how to feel.
Her heart was subdued,
and wanted her life less than death.

30. SMALL TALK

He and I often share various moments of comfortable silence.
Today, I asked him to break the silence,
as we watch the setting sun,
he was smoking his last cigarette:
"do you have any regrets?"
comes a quick answer;
"no"
another silence
"I wish we can live forever though"
"I would like that too."
and the sun sets and his cigarette burns out.

31. A DROP OF ABSINTHE

An element of surprise.
A hint of amusement.
A jolt of wonder.
A rush of excitement.
A dash of romance.
A drop of absinthe.

32. MY YEARNING THOUGHTS

Wish i could say,
wish you could stay.
Wish i could make you feel,
how much you mean to me.

33. HUMMING ON MY OWN TUNE

"This is exactly where i am supposed to be"
I think to myself.
Out on terrace,
under the moonlight,
swaying with the wind,
humming on my own tune.

34. PAIN AND SCAR

Causing pain to yourself
won't heal your scars.

35. EYES...

They told me
beauty lies in the eyes of beholder
yet i see nothing in the eyes that see me.

36. CIGARETTE BUD

I feel like a cigarette bud
taken support of, when low.
thrown away when all high.

37. AND IT ALL MAKE SENSE NOW

Things make so much sense now
when i am standing on that same lane.

38. DROWNING IN THE OCEAN

I see my heart drowning
in the ocean of my tears.

39. BELIEVE

Believe so hard that
even the hardest softens.

40. WORTH THE WAIT

The only thing worth waiting for in life is
when they are not veiled with false hopes and promises.

41. WHO YOU WANT ME TO BE

Why my flaws feels heavier when you are around?

Why do i have to hold my emotions and spill out what you want to hear?

Is it because i try to be who you want me to be?

42. MY ONLY INTENTION

Replacing those pillows with your arms and your warmth
that protects me from the cold breeze are myonly intentions,
with you and me in one picture frame,
growing through all shades of ages together are my only intention.

43. NOT VERY COMFORTABLE

"I don't feel very comfortable."
"why? what happened?"
I feel like there's a hand around my neck
that's dragging me to death.

44. FATHER'S LAP

The day her heart was broken,
she detached herself from everything and left her heart unspoken.
she was upset and in pain,
blamed herself that she must be insane,
then one day after crossing several lanes she finally reached home.
she was tired so she slept on her father's lap,
so that after a long time she can have a sound nap.
soon that horrific episode seemed blur,
and she realized

45. MEMORIES NEVER FADE

Time passed but those memories didn't fade
though after daily race my heart still aches for that same shade,
do not hold the cloud of pain
just cry and let your emotions rain,
it is not easy to let go every single thing
but what is the point of holding things that is only being a cause of
suffering.
just take into account that you struck a match and ignited a blaze,
but never let it burn your grace..

46. THE LAST SIP OF MY WINE

Under the night sky with twinkling stars,
with a glass of wine and you playing my favourite song on your guitar.
an hour passed and the way you insisted me to finish my wine before the
song reaches to it's very end.
i was curious so i drank the last sip and i saw a beautiful ring settled on
the bottom..
for once i thought it was a dream so i blinked thrice and each time i
found you closer and closer.

47. SET YOURSELF FREE

Do not hold your breath for anyone,
do not let your lungs be still
let the blood flow through your veins.
do not haunt yourself to death by recollecting those thoughts
and walking on the same memory lane again
like how easily after giving you scars they asked you to embrace it.
hey you, yes you, whoever is reading this.
stop blaming yourself for the things you never did,
stop driving yourself crazy.
it may delay the cracks from spreading,
but eventually they will.
sometimes to keep yourself together
you must allow yourself to leave,
even if suffering and dealing with things alone..
is what it takes you to breathe.

48. FLY HIGH

I am not really into your world of lies,
and i am not ready to be treated the same
way how people stamp the flies,
instead now i choose to fly high..

49. THE WITHERED ROSE

When reality keeps us apart,
you are still in my dream.
when each page of my book searches for that withered rose,
that makes me gleam.
your love is indeed spiritual not physical,
it seems.

50. WILD HEARTS

Wrapped up in one blanket with your fingers untangling my hair,
and our wild hearts loaded with love,
ready to blend into thick air.

51. RHYTHMS

I don't feel the rhythms of the love songs anymore...
are they off beat or out of trend?

52. HEART, NOT A TEMPORARY RESIDENCE

If your intension was never to stay then it would have been better if you would not have let my heart turn into a temporary residence for you...

53. CHRYSALIS TO BUTTERFLY

I want the dead chrysalis inside me come alive.
turning into beautiful butterflies,
I know that i am holding a storm inside and that's making me colder
with each passing day.
that is the reason i want to set myself free,
from all the chains of pain because
I know
I know how tough it is to rise every morning even when my body aches....

54. WIPE YOUR TEARS

Sleepless disturbing nights,
tears soaked pillow,
a heavy heart full of pain and craving for care,
grow up girl you only need to wipe your tears.

55. OLD SOUL

Burn me to ashes,

tear me into pieces,

wreck me against the hardest stone,

scar me from skin to bones,

cut me open to bleeding,

stop me from breathing,

do not you worry, just one of those death things,

end this thrive, posion my life,

murder my heart but you already know it is cause,

getting a thought of giving my life a pause.

crying and bleeding everyday from inside

but acting as if everything is fine.

every minute, every second a blizzard of thoughts come and hit me hard,

but in some corners of my heart i still wanna live and see myself the way i

was.

56. LOCKSCREEN

She doesn't want a diamond embedded gemstone,
rather she would love to see her picture on your lockscreen.

57. STORYLINE

Why there have to be a time when one of us step back and the other one
just hold on tight?
Why can't the storyline for once feel absolutely right?

58. GAZE

Should i skip my work and just get high gazing at you?

59. WONDERING?

60. TWIRL

I wanna stay up
at night a little longer
and twirl on that old piano tunes.

61. MY MAIL NEWSLETTERS

"*I planned to make my email newsletters more regular where I could attach those files which has been piled up in dust in the trash bin of my heart more than a year,*

I tried! I really did. But the moment I try releasing it, it either shows no attachment or else there's a sudden voice that echoes in my mind that says: You can't make a silk purse out of a sow's ear.

I stopped…I stopped the moment it asked for the sender's name followed by the call of action,

The sound of typing on the keyboard stopped as out of tears I got my vision blurred and I couldn't see the keys of 'Enter, Swift, Addition and Subtraction.'

There was a line that popped on the screen that said 'Link to web-based version',

I didn't know what to do and somehow, I ended up clicking the 'Unsubscribe option.'

I guess even my destiny didn't want me to fall weak and go back attaching those same files that was only an amalgamation of darkness and lie,

So, I cancelled the email, took a deep breath, shut my eyes and now was left with only dream and that was to fly high…."

62. FRAGRANCE

I can still detect your fragrance through my bones.

63. LYRIC

And suddenly all the sad songs are about you.
with each lyric cutting into the wounds etched by you.
and every note breathing you into me.
i sigh in between the pauses to feel alive,
to heave my soul from the guilt of you..
maybe that's why i keep the songs on loop.

64. POEM WITH NO RHYME

Maybe we had to get part,
maybe you were never mine.
maybe it was part of our destiny,
maybe our poems weren't meant to rhyme.

65. ALL CONSUMED

I drink and smoke to numb my senses.
I know what'll it do to me.
the same thing that you did.
came closer while i was vulnerable..
made me confused at first.
gave me joy in the second.
then left me numb.
and now slowly consuming me everyday.

66. CHANGE CAN BE BEAUTIFUL, BUT A SCARY PROCESS

Change can be beautiful and scary at the same time. You can be hurt and wondering what tomorrow will bring, but you can also be healing and be happy. Sometimes it's best not to question why you're feeling this way because there're certain things that cannot be expressed in words so it's better to experience and accept all the emotional changes that comes on our way. And yes, Change can be beautiful, but a scary process....

67. IT'S NEVER TOO LATE

There's still time it's never too late,
Sometimes you may feel like your life is touched by the fickle finger of fate.
But hold on my friend,
This is not your lives dead-end.
This time is just gloomy,
So, don't underestimate your potential because you are not less than a
tsunami.
Soon there will be a clear blue sky,
And you'll be apple of one's eye…

68. CHOKED DOWN

There are thousand thoughts that cross my mind every minute, every second.
And it's not easy for me faking as if everything is fine.
It's choking me I feel like there's a hand around my neck that's dragging me to death.
Sitting in one corner of my room thinking why my life is being such a mess.
Crying and weeping low so that my voice cannot be heard out of the door...
The next day comes but my battery of happiness is still low.
I was breaking myself into bite-sized pieces as I found myself powerless to speak my heart out and was drowning in the thoughts that I never shared...

69. REST

Some might say,
"You've be tough, you can't be weak.
You've to keep fighting to make things work, no matter what."
My thoughts…
If you truly believe in yourself, you'll never lose your shine.
Remember it's okay if you find yourself weak at certain situations, it's okay
if you cry out aloud and it's okay to take a step back to revive yourself…
Rest is as important as working hard.

70. BROKEN PIECES OF YESTERDAY

Finally, it's time to set your heart free and stop looking for happiness in the same place where you lost it. Let the memories fade away with time because life is too short to start your day with broken pieces of yesterday. When the right person comes along, in their eyes, the most beautiful things about you will be who you are as a person. To them, it will be the little things you never think about that made you so amazing.

And on the ashes of yesterday the flower of your new life will bloom…

71. LET'S REWRITE OUR STORY

Can't we rewrite our story into a new and neat one?

72. SHHHH…

Shhhh there's a lot of noise in my head,
Umm…I guess that's the reason I can barely hear my heartbeat…

73. NEVER SETTLE FOR LESS THAN WHAT YOU DESERVE

My dear beautiful, strong soul…
Loving someone whole heartedly is great. But compromising with your
self-respect is not right.
Blaming yourself every time to hide his mistake is not right.
Swallowing all his lies without uttering even a single word only because
that would make him upset is not right.
Please Stop.
Please…
You don't deserve this.
Stop letting him take your love for granted.
Stop settling for temporary pleasures. You are worth more than late night
texts and an uncommitted soul.
You just have to say to yourself,
"I'm not willing to accept anything less than I deserve!
I'm the genuine article!
I'm no less than a graceful picture!
And I deserve to be happy!"
So, never settle for less than what you deserve…

74. ICE TO WATER

*Currently I'm as cold as a frozen chunk, but in the right hands
I'll melt…*

75. LOVE: AN AMALGAMATION OF BOTH PERFECTIONS AND IMPERFECTIONS

Love is the most beautiful feeling that exists and the best feeling that one could ever experience.

Love is a package which not only full of goodies and perfection but is also wrapped and decorated with your flaws and imperfection.

Love can make every flight of imagination turn real.

I can see galaxies in your eyes and a blaze of fire in your hair.

I can see those tracks on your palms and oh my world your smile, loaded with happiness and adventure ready to command for a surgical strike in my heart…

76. LET IT BE SIMPLE: KINDA OLD-FASHION FREAK

You may call me an Old-fashioned freak but this is how it is.

I would love it when you pick flowers and place them on my hair with some beautiful yellow and green leaves on it rather than an expensive bouquet.

In the world where people prefer to watch Netflix and chill. I would love if we could go for a walk holding each other's hand like it's a promise of togetherness forever.

It would be so great if you bring breakfast in bed with a kiss on my forehead and just cherish each other's presence.

My point is…

Don't make love so complicated. Let it be simple, stop trying to make it appear only as a perfect relation.

Set it free.

And stop ranking it on the scale of one, two and three…

77. TRUTH

I still wanna count on those days of our togetherness as the truth.

78. I SUPPOSE

Is it really cold outside?
Or I suppose the cold breeze is intentionally teasing and reminding me of
your absence....

79. HICCUPS

Were you thinking about me?
Umm… I just had hiccups and it stopped only after spelling your name.

80. NOSTALGIA

Nostalgia is like a lily of the valley, beautiful but deadly.

81. BUBBLE

Was that love or just a dare,
Left it it it soaked me all over.
With passing time all you did is dilluted every bit of my emotions and let
it burst like soapy bubble...

82. THE WAY YOU WERE DESIGNED

Be the one who you want to be,

Not the one everyone expects you to be.

God makes no mistakes. If you look at it from that perspective, you will

see that you are a perfect creation of what he intended when he created

you.

Be proud of who you are.

After all, you're not only a one in a million…you're a once in a lifetime.

Be strong and vulnerable as these chains could never hold someone like

you.

I think it is time to finally set yourself free…

83. STRANGERS?

What if our hearts just remained strangers?

84. EYES DO GRASP CONVERSATION

Your lips were still but your eyes said it all.

85. LET'S REWRITE OUR STORY

Can't we rewrite our story into a fresh and neat one?

86. CONCEAL

All the stars pleads,
When the sky bleeds.
Gently wispered, take your time and conceal...

87. NIGHTMARE'S DRAWER

When the days are cold and deceased,

The aura turns pale and diseased.

With the dead tree standing still,

The narrow lanes of the streets eco with the screams.

The chained mortals in between the four walls, feared to set a step out,

The fatal night is here where all the sinners crawl.

Soon the darkness overshadows every streak of light,

With the crowd rising as a headless corpse.

All the cards were fold,

The blood runs stale.

The daybreaks and the first light falls through the curtains on the face,

Sweat rolling all over the flesh.

With breaking breaths looked out of the windows,

There where nooding trees and a folk chirping birds all around.

And that's when there was a period on the nightmare's drawer.

88. THAT VERY MOMENT

With slightly raising his eyebrows and a smile on his face,
A question aroused ," Tell me how you feel in this very moment when we
are so close"?

www.ingramcontent.com/pod-product-compliance
Lightning Source LLC
Chambersburg PA
CBHW031753150726
47989CB00006B/2706